A World

Full
of Hope

Remembering Those
Who Have Gone
before Us

POPE FRANCIS

PREFACE BY
Cardinal José Tolentino de Mendonça

Paulist Press
New York / Mahwah, NJ

Cover design by Sharyn Banks
Book design by Lynn Else

Library of Congress Cataloging-in-Publication Data
Names: Francis, Pope, 1936– author.
Title: A wound full of hope : remembering those who have gone before us / Pope Francis ; preface by Cardinal José Tolentino de Mendonça
Other titles: Dolore colmo di Speranza. English
Description: New York/Mahwah, NJ : Paulist Press, 2022. | Includes bibliographical references. | Summary: "A collection of prayers and reflections from Pope Francis about death and the loss of loved ones"—Provided by publisher.
Identifiers: LCCN 2022018981 (print) | LCCN 2022018982 (ebook) | ISBN 9780809156269 (paperback) | ISBN 9780809187881 (ebook)
Subjects: LCSH: Death—Religious aspects—Catholic Church—Meditations. | Death—Prayers and devotions.
Classification: LCC BT825 .F6713 2022 (print) | LCC BT825 (ebook) | DDC 236/.1—dc23/eng/20220613
LC record available at https://lccn.loc.gov/2022018981
LC ebook record available at https://lccn.loc.gov/2022018982

ISBN 978-0-8091-5626-9 (paperback)
ISBN 978-0-8091-8788-1 (e-book)

Published by Paulist Press
997 Macarthur Boulevard
Mahwah, New Jersey 07430
www.paulistpress.com

Printed and bound in the
United States of America

There is a mysterious solidarity in Christ
between those who have already passed to
the other life and we pilgrims in this one: our
deceased loved ones continue to take care of us
from Heaven. They pray for us, and we pray for
them and we pray with them.

—Pope Francis

Preface

Laudato Si' *through our Sister Death*

It is known how, in his Canticle of the Creatures, Saint Francis of Assisi calls the sun and the stars, the wind and the clouds, the water and the fire brothers and sisters. But only twice in this poem does he use the possessive, to say not "sister" but "our sister." The first is when Francis refers to the earth: "*Laudato si'* [Praise be to you], my Lord, through our Sister Mother Earth, / who sustains and governs us, / and who produces various fruit with colored flowers and herbs." The second time is when he speaks of death: "*Laudato si'*, my Lord, through our Sister Bodily Death, / from whom no one living can escape." Earth and death, in fact, are two very defining experiences; the core of our humanity is substantial. We are earthly creatures and beings destined to pass through the experience of death.

Thinking about death, therefore, corresponds to embracing life in its global mystery. Death has always been with us and accompanies us, even if we don't realize it. A beautiful page of this book that the reader has in his hands is the one in which Pope Francis reminds us of the need to confront ourselves, each of us, with the horizon of our own death: "In this pre-sunset of today, each of us can consider the sunset of one's life: What will my sunset be like? We will all have a sunset, everyone! Do I look at it with hope? Do I look at it with that joy of being welcomed by the Lord?" The Holy Father presents an existential and faith journey that needs to be pursued.

Accepting death by preparing oneself internally

The poet Paul Celan wrote:

Death is a flower that blooms only once.
Yet as it blooms, it doesn't bloom like
    anything else.
It blooms when it wants, it doesn't bloom
    in time.
It comes, a huge moth, decorating the
    swaying stalk.
You let me be a stalk, so strong it makes
    him happy.

It is very true, as the poem notes: death is a flower that blooms when it wants, even when one would not say that its season has arrived. But Celan insists on a very important aspect spiritually that it is up to us to take on as our task: the familiarity that each of us is called to create, throughout life, with one's own death. If we pay attention to it, it "comes, a huge moth, decorating the swaying stalk."

There really is an inevitable relationship that each of us must work on regarding the horizon of our own death. The biblical texts of wisdom frequently insist: "Man, remember that you are mortal;" "Man, transform the fact that your days are numbered into a fountain of wisdom" (see Ps 90:12). Similarly, the Holy Father declares in the post-synodal apostolic exhortation *Amoris laetitia*: "If we accept death, we can prepare ourselves for it" (no. 258).

Our hope in the face of death

This does not mean that we will not be able, at one time or another, to remove the tension that the thought of death produces in us, nor does it mean that death must become painless or that we must become indifferent to it. Death remains one of the most serious issues in life—a question that we do not know how to illuminate and resolve, without the christological key. The Pope rightly expresses himself in this volume: "The grave is the place where no one who enters ever leaves. But Jesus emerged for us; he rose for us, to bring life where there was death, to begin a new story in the very place where a stone had been placed." And for this reason, the Successor of Peter can say, confirming our faith, "Jesus himself will come to each of us and take us by the hand, with his tenderness, his meekness, his love....This is our hope in the face of death." Easter challenges us to believe that life is greater than death and that the God announced by Jesus of Nazareth is the God of Life. We are not mere spectators of the resurrection of Jesus: we are involved, inscribed in this radical mystery of love that subtracts human history from fate and redeems it.

Living in mourning. Rediscovering communion

Talking about death is also talking about mourning. Indeed, to consider our death is as much or even more painful than to suffer the death of those we love. The pain of separation is greater than any word. The tears of Jesus in front of the tomb of his dead friend speak of the pain of separation: "When Mary reached where Jesus was, as soon as she saw him, she threw herself at his feet saying: 'Lord, if you had been here, my brother would not have died.' Then, when Jesus saw her weeping and the Jews who had come with her also weep, he was deeply moved and, very upset, he asked: 'Where have you placed him?' They said to him: 'Lord, come and see!' Jesus burst into tears. Then the Jews said: 'See how he loved him!'" (John 11:32–36).

A touching testimony comes from ancient Christianity through the close friendship of two important theologians of the fourth century, Gregory of Nazianzus and Basil the Great. Meditating on their binding affection, Gregory often wrote that he seemed to have with his friend a single soul in two bodies. And in lamenting Basil's death, he left us one of the most realistic descriptions of what mourning represents: "If someone had told me that a body can live without its own soul, I would have believed him. But not that I could live without you." It is really impossible to live without others. The absence of those we love will continue to hurt us until the end. And until the end, we will continue to elaborate this emptiness inwardly, which we will then discover to be not only emptiness but also superabundance, even companionship, even a mysterious form of communion. With an exhortation that is always opportune, Pope Francis challenges us, in the experience of mourning, to look twice. Certainly, looking at the wound within us that is caused by the death of those we love. But, at the same time, not to cease to look up, to look beyond. As he writes, "This is the strength that hope gives us."

—*Cardinal José Tolentino de Mendonça*

~ 1 ~

Hope is a little like leaven that expands our souls. There are difficult moments in life, but with hope the soul goes forward and looks ahead to what awaits us. Today is a day of hope. Our brothers and sisters are in the presence of God, and we shall also be there, through the pure grace of the Lord, if we walk along the way of Jesus.

Visit to the Redipuglia War Memorial,
Fogliano Redipuglia, September 13, 2014.

2

Today, in remembrance of many brothers and sisters who have passed on, it will do us good to look at the cemeteries and to look heavenward. And to repeat, like Job: "I know that my Redeemer lives, and I myself will see him. My eyes shall behold him, and not another." And this is the strength that hope gives us, this freely given gift that is the virtue of hope. May the Lord give it to all of us.

3

*E*ven death trembles when a Christian prays, because it knows that everyone who prays has an ally who is stronger than it: the Risen Lord.

Visit to the tomb of Don Lorenzo Milani,
Barbiana, June 20, 2017.

4

Our loved ones have not disappeared into the darkness of nowhere: hope assures us that they are in the good and strong hands of God. Love is stronger than death. This is why the way is to make love grow, make it more solid, and love will guard us until the day when every tear is dried, when "there will be no more death, no mourning, no lamentation, no pain" (Rev 21:4). If we allow ourselves to be supported by this faith, the experience of mourning can generate a stronger solidarity of family ties, a new openness to the pain of other families, a new fraternity with families that are born and are reborn in hope. Being born and reborn in hope, this gives us faith.

~ 5 ~

Praying for the dead is, first and foremost, a sign of appreciation for the witness they have left us and the good that they have done. It is giving thanks to the Lord for having given them to us and for their love and their friendship....It is a simple, effective, meaningful remembrance because it entrusts our loved ones to God's mercy. We pray with Christian hope that they may be with him in Paradise, as we wait to be together again in that mystery of love which we do not comprehend, but which we know to be true because it is a promise that Jesus made. We will all rise again and we will all be forever with Jesus, with Him.

6

All of us will experience sundown, all of us! Do we look at it with hope? Do we look with that joy at being welcomed by the Lord? This is a Christian thought that gives us hope. Today is a day of joy; however, it is serene and tranquil joy, a peaceful joy. Let us think about the passing away of so many of our brothers and sisters who have preceded us, let us think about the evening of our life, when it will come. And let us think about our hearts and ask ourselves: "Where is my heart anchored?" If it is not firmly anchored, let us anchor it beyond, on that shore, knowing that hope does not disappoint because the Lord Jesus does not disappoint.

~ 7 ~

*P*rayer for the deceased, raised in the trust that they dwell with God, extends its benefits to us too: it educates us in a true vision of life; it opens us up to true freedom, disposing us to the continuous search for eternal goods.

Visit to the Verano Monumental Cemetery,
Rome, November 1, 2014.

— 8 —

Jesus himself will come to each of us and take us by the hand, with his tenderness, his meekness, his love. Each one repeat Jesus' words in your heart: "Arise, come. Arise, come. Arise, rise again!" This is our hope in the face of death. For those who believe, it is a door that is thrust open wide; for those who doubt it is a glimmer of light that filters through an exit that is not quite completely closed. But for all of us it will be a grace, when this light, of the encounter with Jesus, illuminates us.

～ 9 ～

*B*y contemplating Christ's union with the Father even at the height of his sufferings on the cross (see Mark 15:34), Christians learn to share in the same gaze of Jesus. Even death is illumined and can be experienced as the ultimate call to faith, the ultimate "Go forth from your land" (Gen 12:1), the ultimate "Come!" spoken by the Father, to whom we abandon ourselves in the confidence that he will keep us steadfast even in our final passage.

~ 10 ~

Jesus illuminated this mystery of our death. By his example, he permits us to grieve when a dear person passes on. He is "deeply" troubled at the tomb of his friend Lazarus, and "wept" (John 11:35). Here, Jesus' demeanor makes us feel very close to him, our brother. He wept for his friend Lazarus. Then Jesus prays to the Father, wellspring of life, and commands Lazarus to come out of the tomb. And so it happens. Christian hope draws from Jesus' approach to human death: if it is present in creation, it is nonetheless an affront that tarnishes God's loving plan, which the Savior wishes to remove for our sake.

11

God of Jesus, our Father who art in heaven. Thanks to Him, the crucified and Risen One, we know that your name, "God of Abraham, God of Isaac, God of Jacob," means that you are not God of the dead but of the living (see Matt 22:32), that your covenant of steadfast love is mightier than death and is a guarantee of resurrection.

~ 12 ~

Of all the things that we have collected, all that we have saved, we will bring nothing with us...except we will carry the embrace of the Lord. Thinking about your death, you may wonder, "Will I die? When?" It is not set in the calendar but the Lord knows it. Pray to the Lord, "Lord, prepare my heart to die well, to die in peace, to die with hope." This is the word that must always accompany our life, the hope of living with the Lord here and then living with the Lord somewhere else. We pray for this for each other.

13

By his wounds we have been healed (see 1 Pet 2:24), the apostle Peter says, by his death we have been reborn, all of us. And thanks to him, abandoned on the cross, no one will ever again be alone in the darkness of death. Never, he is always beside us: we need only open our heart and let ourselves be looked upon by him.

Visit to the Verano Monumental Cemetery,
Rome, November 1, 2014.

~ 14 ~

How many good people have we met and do we know, about whom we say: "This person is a saint!"? These are the saints next door, those who are not canonized but who live with us. Imitating their gestures of love and mercy is a bit like perpetuating their presence in this world. These evangelical gestures are indeed the only ones that can withstand the destruction of death: an act of tenderness, generous aid, time spent listening, a visit, a kind word, a smile....In our eyes these gestures might seem insignificant, but in the eyes of God they are eternal, because love and compassion are stronger than death.

15

If we look at things from only a human per-spective, we tend to say that man's journey moves from life to death. This is what we see! But this is only so if we look at things from a human perspective. Jesus turns this perspective upside down and states that our pilgrimage goes from death to life: the fullness of life! We are on a journey, on a pilgrimage toward the fullness of life, and that fullness of life is what illumines our journey!

Visit to the Redipuglia War Memorial,
Fogliano Redipuglia, September 13, 2014.

~ 16 ~

We are called to take away the stones of all that suggests death: for example, the hypocrisy with which faith is lived, is death; the destructive criticism of others, is death; insults, slander, are death; the marginalization of the poor, is death. The Lord asks us to remove these stones from our hearts, and life will then flourish again around us. Christ lives, and those who welcome him and follow him come into contact with life. Without Christ, or outside of Christ, not only is life not present, but one falls back into death.

~ 17 ~

Remembering the dead, caring for their graves and prayers of suffrage, are the testimony of confident hope, rooted in the certainty that death does not have the last word on human existence, for man is destined to a life without limits, which has its roots and its fulfillment in God.

~ 18 ~

If we accept death, we can prepare ourselves for it. The way is to grow in our love for those who walk at our side, until that day when "death will be no more, mourning and crying and pain will be no more" (Rev 21:4). We will thus prepare ourselves to meet once more our loved ones who have died. Just as Jesus "gave back to his mother" (see Luke 7:15) her son who had died, so it will be with us. Let us not waste energy by dwelling on the distant past. The better we live on this earth, the greater the happiness we will be able to share with our loved ones in heaven. The more we are able to mature and develop in this world, the more gifts will we be able to bring to the heavenly banquet.

19

*J*esus bore our humanity and brought it beyond death to a new place, to Heaven, so that there where He is, we might also be.

Visit to Laurentino Cemetery,
Rome, November 2, 2018.

20

Today we glimpse our future and we celebrate what we were born for: we were born so as to die no more; we were born to enjoy God's happiness! The Lord encourages us and says to those setting out on the path of the Beatitudes: "Rejoice and be glad, for your reward is great in heaven" (Matt 5:12).

21

The grave is the place where no one who enters ever leaves. But Jesus emerged for us; he rose for us, to bring life where there was death, to begin a new story in the very place where a stone had been placed. He, who rolled away the stone that sealed the entrance of the tomb, can also remove the stones in our hearts. So, let us not give in to resignation; let us not place a stone before hope. We can and must hope, because God is faithful. He did not abandon us; he visited us and entered into our situations of pain, anguish and death. His light dispelled the darkness of the tomb: today he wants that light to penetrate even to the darkest corners of our lives. Dear sister, dear brother, even if in your heart you have buried hope, do not give up: God is greater. Darkness and death do not have the last word. Be strong, for with God nothing is lost!

22

"God so loved the world" (John 3:16). It truly is a love so tangible, so tangible that he took our death upon himself. To save us, he went there, to where we had ended up, separating ourselves from God the giver of life: in death, in a sepulcher with no way out. This is the debasement that the Son of God fulfilled, bending down to us as a servant in order to take on all that is ours, until opening wide the doors of life.

~ 23 ~

Jesus teaches us to live with life's pain by accepting the reality of life with trust and hope, putting the love of God and neighbor first even in our suffering: It is love that transforms everything.

Visit to the American Cemetery,
Nettuno, November 2, 2017.

24

When so many times in history men think of waging a war, they are convinced they are bringing about a new world; they are convinced they are creating a "springtime." And it ends in a dreadful, cruel winter, with the reign of terror and death. Today let us pray for all the departed, all of them, but in a special way for these young people, at a moment in which so many die in the daily battles of this piecemeal war. Let us also pray for today's dead, the victims of war, also children, innocents. This is the result of war: death. May the Lord grant us the grace to weep.

25

We all have an appointment with God in the night, in the night of our life...We need not fear: because God will give us a new name, which contains the meaning of our entire life; he will change our heart and will offer us the blessing reserved to those who have allowed themselves to be changed by him. This is a beautiful invitation to allow ourselves to be changed by God. He knows how to do so because he knows each one of us.

~ 26 ~

In this time of uncertainty and anguish, I invite everyone to welcome the gift of hope that comes from Christ. It is He who helps us navigate the tumultuous waters of sickness, death, and injustice, which do not have the last word over our final destination.

27

Our life is made of time and time is God's gift, and it is therefore important to make use of it by performing good and fruitful actions.

Visit to the Fosse Ardeatine,
Rome, November 2, 2017.

~ 28 ~

We have a great challenge to face, especially in contemporary culture, which often tends to trivialize death to the point of treating it as an illusion or hiding it from sight. Yet death must be faced and prepared for as a painful and inescapable passage, yet one charged with immense meaning, for it is the ultimate act of love toward those we leave behind and toward God whom we go forth to meet.

29

The resurrection of Jesus tells us that the last word does not belong to death, but to life. By resurrecting His only begotten Son, God the Father fully manifested His love and mercy for humanity for all time. If Christ is risen, we can feel confident in every moment of our existence, even those times that are the most difficult and full of anguish and uncertainty.

30

In Jesus, God gives us eternal life, he gives it to everyone, and thanks to him everyone has the hope of a life even truer than this one. The life that God prepares for us is not a mere embellishment of the present one: it surpasses our imagination, for God continually amazes us with his love and with his mercy.

Visit to the Prima Porta Cemetery,
Rome, September 2, 2016.